RESOLUTION:

Tears of Joy

- Promise Fulfilled

~

Sequel to

Tears of Stone and My Deal with God

First Edition

ISBN 978-0-9987395-3-3

Published by Estherleon Schwartz

Contact: estherleon@estherleon.com
www.estherleon.com

Cover mural by Mear One

Book design and typesetting by Michael Rosen

Printed in the United States of America

Also By The Author:

Tears Of Stone and My Deal With God
Simply Meditate
Simply Meditate with Your Dog And Meow
Simply Meditate with Giggles

July 4th 2021...

Never say NEVER.
Here we go again to continue the saga of
Tears Of Stone And My Deal With God.
Written long ago on my old computer with determination
and fervor. I had never written a book before.
One morning I woke up, went to the bathroom
and came out thanking God,
'cause I knew what it feels like the rest of the day
if the prunes, prune juice, and Metamucil didn't respond.
I opened a Word document and felt it saying, "Go for it."
My fingers went faster then my thoughts,
as if my fingers were my thoughts,
before my thoughts...in total control.
No, I am not on drugs, had my 3 zips of coffee
and it became a book, embraced at Barnes and Noble.
"This is now," I said in a whisper.
Will I have the passion, the 'want' to write some more,
as I am writing right this minute on July 4th, 2021 at 12:53pm
to continue, and why, for what, for whom...
I thought back where it all began.

And Then...
THANK YOU CREEPO CORONA VIRUS
I became the journalist that I'm not.
FINALLY THE WORLD STOOD STILL
AND CAME TOGETHER...
It all began many, many years ago when I got my coffee
in the morning, had 3 zips and then it happened.
I never questioned the coffee inspiration hype (was just in awe).
And when I came home and looked at my computer,
'WORD DOCUMENT' stared at me
and I felt it said, "Then what?"
It reminded me when my cousin said to me,
in the hospital, getting chemotherapy,
"Esty, what happened to you during the Holocaust?"
I visited her every day and she said, "Then what?"
I started to tell her the beginnings of my life
and I started to type.

Actually I kept typing and typing and looked so forward
to sharing with her, and she would always say,
"Then what? Then what happened?"
It became an inspiration to type one more page,
one more page, one more page, now page 129...
me coming to America, as a child Holocaust survivor,
I kept writing and before you know it, 'it' became a book called,
Tears Of Stone and My Deal With God.
What was really, really a sort of miracle,
BARNES AND NOBLE took it on.
I am a self-publisher, meaning no representation,
means be prepared to promote yourself,
which means I did not have the funds.
Which means do your very best
and let God take care of the rest.

I am a Cantor, one who sings prayers.
So it was, and always is the most 'High'.
And my mother, father and Sam, my brother,
and Ivor Pyres (you will get to know him)
as well as some very close friends
who believed in something higher kept saying,
"So, what happened then?"
I know they, my true friends of pure souls
helped me from 'up there' and then out of nowhere,
truly, after the routine of 3 zips of coffee in the morning,
I started a series of tiny meditation books,
very colorful covers (color matters big time)
to carry around with you in your purse, anything that has pockets.
Yes, those words, "What happened then?"
were my inspiration and support.

Then out of nowhere came the plague, AKA: Corona virus.
Ivor Pyres, my best male friend and singing partner in duets,
kept saying to me even before the plague,
CREEPO CORONA VIRUS, write another book.
I said "I'm done with writing books that are just sitting there
reminding me you need representation
and 'moolah' ($) and felt I have written
my thoughts and feelings down and have
no more desire to write about anything into book form.
Who knew, but 'The Shadow', that the 'COFFEE HYPE'
was in cahoots with the PLAGUE?
They had a conspiracy for me to continue
this story of revealing injustice
affecting the underprivileged, the orphans, the poor...

Maybe this time unknowingly, subconsciously
something in our higher consciousness was saying, "Enough."
Just maybe this time, we will not go back to unjust,
unholy ways. Hopefully this time there will be
a reverence, to not abuse the beautiful green earth,
and feel the wisdom of a tree when you hug it.
We were born pure souls, to care,
to have compassion, to have mercy
and walk a path of doing the 'right thing', to be useful.
This is one's worth, is it not?
This plague and other plagues of the past
have brought out the pure soul of caring,
as we see the actions of humanity coming together.
SOS, to help beyond words of creativity,
imagination in bringing all breathing peoples together
and yes, animals looking at us,
perhaps praying and saying,
"Look into our eyes."
There is something so beautiful in all animals' eyes.
I see the soul of God.

This virus has a message.
March 2021
California, where I live, was ordered to:
Stay at Home
Wear masks when out
Only go for groceries and bare necessities
and wash hands every inch of the way.
So now I went to Starbucks for my morning hype
and it had that note on the door, like every other store:

DUE TO THE CORONA VIRUS
WE ARE TEMPORARILY CLOSED FOR WALK IN

WHAT? They would never close, in my mind,
unless it burned down.
Am I dreaming all this? I do have nightmares,
have a touch of Parkinson's, (they say you can become delusional),
have delayed reactions to life's challenges,
as I immediately go into action mode
and emotionally catch up later,
maybe a bit melodramatic when I do story telling.
Do I care? No. Been there, done that.

7

The parking lot is empty. Where are the faces I see every day,
walking with their dogs, wagging their tails as I pet them?
The routine of throwing on my oversized coat, dark shades,
and hair cover-up, thinking about the baristas,
saying, "Hey, how is you?" And me saying, "Hey,"
throwing kisses upward and we both smile.
That is my morning wake up call to the world
as I zip my 3 zips with yummie half and half steamed milk.
I walked 200 feet to Melrose, not a soul in sight,
no cars driving. I must be dreaming.
Please God, wake me up. Am I in the Twilight Zone?
Or is this the Apocalypse, the only person left -
little ole me - reminding me of one of my favorite movies,
The Book of Eli, made into a movie, which I watch
whenever on TV, always like the first time.

Wake up Esther, wake up. I AM UP.
OK, where can I find a cup of coffee?
I kept walking on Melrose,
no familiar faces with dogs wagging their tails,
no cars, only birds, humming and the sky so blue
were my clues that this is for real.
As I whistle to the birds, they whistle back,
so I have witnesses that I am not hallucinating.
(I will record this and put it up on YouTube)

I saw a sign across the street on the wall: COFFEE.
OK, a sign, a good sign, as I'm into signs. You too?
I went in, they had just opened a few months ago
and were very welcoming.
I ordered a short cup of coffee, trying to explain
only 3/4 coffee and the rest very foamy half and half.
I guess they call that a Misto, my daughter, Carrie, told me
the times we were together...
And I still had to explain it in detail.
Why can't I just order a Misto?
I looked around, took my 3 zips, about 30 seconds
I got my 'high' and then it came to me,
the chatter in my head said,
"Take a selfie for evidence that you are
not in the Twilight Zone, girl."

That was my 'wake up' call
and I started taking pictures
on my morning walk.
The only pictures I ever took
were 'selfies' to send to Dani, my granddaughter,
to check out my new hair color
and see if she approved.
Now, I somehow feel I need to do this,
take pictures, and write the story of my relationship
with these photos, with the world.
The chatter in my head said, "Then what?"
Well, the next day I got up,
made my bed with love and gratitude
(before I even went to the bathroom).
Leaving the bathroom,
I looked upward and said
a thousand thank you's
and of course threw kisses upward.

I always remembered when I visited patients
in the hospital and did singing prayers with them,
tubes coming out from all parts of their body,
I turned around, blew a kiss to them and they smiled.
I got a lump in my throat, the chatter in my head said,
"Thank you, God." That is why when I leave the bathroom
I am so grateful that I can do my thing,
without tubes, you know what I mean?
Actually there are gratitude prayers for everything
and it sure helps my soul when I remember that and do them,
even just for my breath, a reminder that was breathed into me
when I was born, now always in gratitude,
especially since I started a Music Meditation,
focused on our life line, 'the breath.'

I am Grateful

I am Grateful

I am Grateful

I am Grateful

Every day with a mask,
walking and seeing unfamiliar faces here and there
giving one another a high sign.
Gee, how sweet is that?
I felt connected even tho I never saw them before
or maybe it is the mask and baseball cap incognito,
it really does not matter.
The fact that I thought I did not know them,
yet was greeted with such heart,
the pure soul of a human being,
all this, like never before,
on the way to find
another coffee café open.
I saw a sweet friendly café still open,
to spread some neighborhood and gratitude
for being spared from the PLAGUE
and the beating Melrose has endured.

Walking on Fairfax, my Fairfax since 1948...
When I came to America, Fairfax was the home
for immigrants - bakeries, kosher butchers,
Hatikvah music Store, Solomon's gifts,
where I got my Torah, retrieved from the Holocaust.
As my Papa and I walked, especially on Friday,
erev Shabbat, to get a challah at Schwartz' bakery,
(no relationship), kosher wine and other
kosher goodies for Shabbat to share
with the few that survived the Holocaust...since 1948
Men were dressed in suits and a hat,
kind of the look of Humphrey Bogart,
and nodded at one another and said, "Good Shabbos".
They sat on the bus benches and reminisced...
and some just stared at life.
I was 8 years old and to me they were my family, too.
Sometimes my Papa invited those that were
the only survivors, to share our Shabbos meal.
Too sad what happened between 2018 and 2022
to my Fairfax, the hub of the Jewish Community...

So what happened then?
GREED GREED GREED.
Soulless hearts with no consciousness to nurture
this most beautiful earth, created for all breathing beings
and nature and all creatures, from an ant to a dinosaur,
to all that survive in water and the beautiful birds
in the sky, shot down as a 'cool' sporting sport...
Give me a break, that sucks.
And, what about my beautiful Fairfax Avenue?
Greedy landlords, you know who you are,
building religious schools, plastered your name on buildings...
Maybe you forgot who gifted you most of these properties -
your grand parents, immigrants, your parents.
They are crying in their graves because of
their generous hearts, asking God to forgive you
for your lack of compassion that you did not
negotiate something, so that these long term
renters could sustain themselves and
give the community historical history...A LEGACY.

Tell me, is this the way your parents raised you,
is this how you give love and respect to your grandparents?
When did you lose your way?
My precious Fairfax Avenue,
turned into designer stores, especially shoes.
Kids stand around the block, with their wallets out,
anxious to get a pair of designer shoes,
(food for them, like being rationed out).
Do they feel that defines their worth?
And where did they get the $$? These shoes are expensive.
I once asked one of the kids in line,
"Where do you get the money to buy those expensive shoes?"
They replied, "I work a lot of hours."
As a child Holocaust survivor, going to Fairfax High School
in Los Angeles, there is a part of me that gets it,
one feels to be 'in' is to wear designer clothes,
or have that pinky ring and cashmere sweaters.
Ironically, in the 1980s, I founded 13 *House of Cashmere*
stores with my brother, see my previous book,
Tears Of Stone And My Deal With God.

Souls of the Feet, of the Holocaust,
can never be destroyed

And what about the doll store at the mall?
$250.00 for a doll, and people from all walks of life,
maybe spending their last $$
to make their kid happy,
so that their precious child will feel 'they fit in.'
Is this who we are?
Have we lost our way?
So sad, I just imagine the angels weeping
and saying to God, "Give them another chance."
I had none of that. What I had cannot be measured
with all the money and fame in the world.
My best friend was, is forever,
as long as I have breath,
God and my Papa.

These kids are the same kids.
Their best has emerged during the Corona virus,
AKA the Plague, surfaced the true born pure souls,
coming out of their mother's warm womb.
I believe the innate caring, kind, sensitive
person is, who maybe long for within themselves
unknowing...to feel that soul inside.
I went to the manager of one of those "cool" stores
and suggested, what if your next event,
announcing a release of new designer shoes
and asked them to bring a can of food
for the depleted food banks,
would be their admission to get in,
would that not be an eye opener, heart opener,
and transform their minds, becoming
a role model for their generation.

I believe in the youth, to bring wholeness
back to the world again,
like when the pioneers founded America
and gave us doctrines to live by,
doctrines to guide us,
a prayer after reciting the Pledge of Allegiance
to feel some reverence and gratitude.
In spite of it all, I still believe, Anna Frank,
I am thinking so what part of 12 years
since my last book, I have sort of brought you
up to date and now "what happened then"
the chatter in my head said,
"Girl, you sound ungrateful for the gift
I gave you. I spared you, that's why, for what?
To give hope to others and for whom,
for me, your God and his precious people, get it?"
I brought special beings into your life...

That's all I needed to bring me back to a sense of awe,
a strength, a warm feeling in my gut (the truth)
and calling Ivor to confirm what I wrote was OK...
His response, "Keep going, Sweetness."
Yes, lots of Ivor is in my last book.
It never ceases to amaze me, that I am writing again,
A sense of excitement,
especially that I said, "Never again."
One never knows what God has in store for you.
Guys, my creative hands and mind are reaching
out to you, for me to continue to share
the people in my life that shaped me
into who I am at 79 years old,
been there, done that and still around.
Thank you, God

Ivor pulled up on my now Apple computer
tons of written docs I wrote
in the last 10 years, like foot notes,
and I came across something
written by Ivor about me.
I was stunned when I read it.
"So as usual, Esther likes to enlist people
into her field of dreams
even if everybody knows
it's going to be a nightmare.
She sowed the seed, and like a horse
that can smell the water after dying of thirst
in the fields of Los Angeles,
I decided to drink, 'sucker'."

"God, whom she normally evokes,
is privately laughing because he can see
the mayhem that is about to erupt.
But I think he is secretly laughing
because it is creative mayhem.
Like it was when he created the world.
I don't think he was happy with a two-dimensional
world as his color palette and a beret.
Were there any French before the world got created?
Anyway, so he invented 3D printing
before we ever thought of it.
I'm sure he scared himself when he created
some of the ugliest and most destructive
creatures on earth; he was only mixing colors.
So he also created cute things like Esther,
who create the mayhem
that big ugly things do in a different way."

"Anyway I am going to run with this
until it gets boring and then,
like kids in a sand pit,
the sand will look like sand
and not the Arabian castles
we were playing in,
and we will all go home,
coming to visit the sand pit with Esther again
and this time it will be who knows what.
Is this great fun for geriatrics, which we are?
If the seven ages of man are to go back
to being a child again,
get ready to have sand thrown in your face,
which will probably
make you cry because you are not able
to take it at this age of your life.
No use crying to mommy
because she's not around
and didn't have the luxury of playing
in the sand pit with Esther.
Good luck with this."

It's the real deal.

Could you, would you believe this
from my Ivor...is this what he thinks of me?
I was so stunned to think this man
of 18 years on my side (the spiritual side)
that prays with me in public, sings with me
from Puccini to Pop and puts up with
my million phone calls a day...
he answers the phone, "Hi bub, all OK?"
"No Ivor, all is not OK."
"Are you having a bad day with your hair?
I can't believe what you wrote...
I called Gail to vent, she was not home,
I cannot believe what he wrote.
Am I missing something here...
feel free to e-mail me and lend your voice,
so I may understand his Shakespeare response.

Ivor is my mother who I never got
the motherly love from, he is my everything father
that saved me from the Nazi's, he is my brother, Sam
that took his life trying to prove himself to the family.
I feel like my world is upside down
(the chatter in my head, Esther look upward,
like you preach to all around you).
Can a human being turn on you like this?
- like during the Holocaust,
best friends turning on each other...
But he is Ivor that creates magic,
mixes and matches music
into albums like no one else,
well, maybe Puccini, Mozart, Beethoven.
I called him, "Hi, bub."
Ivor: "Don't give me your *Hi, bub.*"
Is this what you feel about me,"
Esther, I paid you the highest respect
comparing you to...

Woke up this morning early, questioning my brain,
my heart; am I really going to continue writing?
Something deep inside reminds me what I said
to the therapist (a good lady, tell you more later).
I just want to be more graceful, strong, reliable,
turn chaos into order that feeds the soul.
To still see a vision for the future,
Ivor came to understand,
and after listening to Jordan Peterson,
a renowned voice in the psychoanalytic world
who respects Jung and Friedrich Nietzsche,
about a moral obligation to keep 'truckin' along'
in purpose and what has meaning to you;
to perfect it's destiny thru your social,
spiritual obligation until
the Divine brings you home.

God bless my grandsons,
Max and Jordan,
who turned me on to these people
and for most, the thought of being
distant from God
would be hell.
Jordan Peterson, I hope you read this,
those words you shared in your video,
reminded me of my love for God...yes, "I'm in."

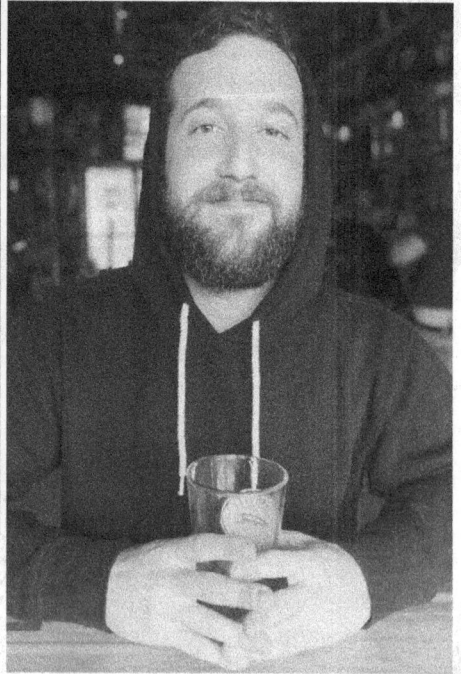

OK Esther, what's the order of the day?
When I wake up in the morning
under the warm covers in my bed,
something in me says,
"Hi, you're still alive."
One can never take anything for granted
in these uncertain times...
Since I wrote my last book in 2009,
Tears Of Stone And My Deal With God,
which to me was surely guided.
I reminisce about what came down
13 years later, and wondering,
am I still the same girl, Esther,
and about it's effects.
I am trying real hard to find the words
to type on my Apple computer that will express
what 'time' can do to one's brain and soul.

First. I'm going to make my bed.
With much care I make my bed
that gives so much to me,
a comfort is always there for me,
like when I don't feel good, want to get into bed,
surely you must feel that way at times...
So the first thing in line of order in the morning
is I make my bed with much love and gratitude...
A visual order and mindful gratitude helps
to view and feel good and better, as in Genesis,
God gave order to a void world and said,
"This is good."
Wow, I am so glad I went to my Torah class
each week and was so in awe
with Rabbi Levy Meir,
as he uttered each word
out of the Torah with such wisdom,
insight, placed on his lips from the divine.
Sharing this with you fills my heart
with so much joy that my memory is working and telling me,
"Esther, all these people, the experiences
have made you more of who you are now, keep writing..."

What does it all mean
when it's all said and done
in an instant,
in a moment,
can it be revealed,
can it be uttered,
to be, or become,
someone else
or the true you?
Am I the past
or am I the present
or am I the future
or am I just experiencing
divine revelations
just to rest under a tree
for more divine revelations,
then perhaps
I found me.

Woke up this morning, hey I'm still alive,
thank you, God, so what's the deal today??
Coffee for starters
(keep writing chatter in my mind)
OK, OK, as usual,
left on my checkered PJ bottom,
tucked into my Uggs,
(something about the fur lining is comforting??)
said, "Hi," to my pilot black oversized jacket,
same yarmulka (kippah) on my head,
turned on computer, said, "See you in 10 (min)."
Said 'Hi,' to David, my son that lives upstairs,
talk to the Magnolia trees,
four of them, named after my four grandchildren,
give them a fast hug
(try it, it works, something just feels gooood).

–Dani

Across the street from my building
there is an orthodox synagogue on the corner,
next to the alley. I hear the prayers,
chanted like my Papa used to do every morning.
I peak in thru the beautiful stained windows
and there they are, with their tallits (prayer shawls)
covering their heads in deep prayer.
Those moments are eternity for me as I sniff
and breathe in the sacredness of it all, feeling so safe,
so happy for that special moment, en route
to Starbucks for my 3 zips of coffee
and to see all the familiar faces
and hear the familiar sounds of the world.

It always amazes me that I feel I have to walk
thru the dirty alley, within 500 feet.
Why am I obsessed to take that route,
with homeless people peeing in the bushes,
yet with pride, not asking for a handout
like in front of Canter's deli
when I meet Lucy for borscht.
There's always the same man, with a beautiful
Godly smile and kind words on his tongue,
"How is you today, Miss?"
When you're 79 and someone calls you 'Miss,'
I reach in my wallet...homeless, and smart.
What is that all about, Esther?
Only the SHADOW KNOWS

Friday, yeaaaaaaaaaa. It's shabbos time.
I still remember when we came to America,
my papa and I would go early Friday morning
to Schwartz' bakery, get challah and kosher wine,
and Papa would say to everyone
with his gentle, loving smile,
"A sweet Shabbos to you."
He always greeted people with such reverence,
always a mini kind of head nod gesture,
that made you feel you're someone special to the world...
He is more than worth reading about,
and how he loved God, in my first book.
I reminisce how we used to sit at the Shabbos table -
my papa at one head and my uncle Michael
on the other end - my whole family quiet,
until my father recited the prayers.
My mother lit the candles, and I felt
at that moment, she, too, loved Shabbos and God.

Thinking about her now, this moment today,
on Friday, May 17th. at 12:28pm
evokes a crying heart for her, too bad
I didn't feel that for her then...
too late to tell her, or is it?
I do believe we stay connected after we pass on,
thru a sign, prayers, talking out loud,
facing upward...I now discuss with my grandchildren
a 'sign' when I am no longer physically here
that they feel I'm listening.

I was at the computer in thought,
actually heavy thought about this thing called life.
I heard some heavy duty scratching on my roof.
I looked up at the skylight and saw these huge images
of black skinny feet trying to rip off the material
that seals the skylight, to get in,
like something out of Hitchcock's movie, *The Birds*.
I ran outside and saw a flock of oversized
black crows talking to each other,
looking at each other and loud screams from me.
My son came running out and said, "What now, Mom?"
It made me feel like I was a pest to him, yet,
he most of the time shows such care,
bringing unexpected food (kosher), as he knows
I don't eat chicken or meat unless it has been blessed,
and even then the idea of slaughtering animals
reminds me of the holocaust and cannibalism.
I truly felt the crows were staring me down.
No, I do not smoke that funny stuff.
I called Ivor about what was coming down and he said,
"Oh, crows are good luck."
He must know, he is from India.

So I Googled spiritual crows,
do they bring good luck?
"Gee," I thought, just before Shabbos
I'm going to get a new insight,
a good message to reflect on.
I started to read about crows.
It said that death is near,
rethink what you are saying and doing,
crows know your face forever.
In short, I felt that satanic forces
have invaded my being and home.
Oh, God, is this a joke or a sign?

Woke up in the morning and, strangely enough,
felt refreshed, and very clear minded.
Hmm, should one literally inhale
and trust the info on the computer?
Maybe some Divine to keep me on track to intervention,
it's Shabbos tonight...
What I haven't shared with you is that
it's not every Cantor's dream
to do their 'God chosen thing'
in the ivory tower temple,
with the ivory tower congregation,
and mucho moola ($)
and not have to sweat out,
will they show up, meaning, will people come?

Bottom line, I chose to do outreach work,
build it and they will come and they did.
I was happy to be the rebel with a cause,
to bring souls back to their roots
and look upward and chit-chat more
with their best friend—God.
And they will live happily ever after.
Who knew the revelations would be at Lenny's Deli,
in between chicken soup (kosher style)
and peoples of all walks of life
came to break bread, AKA Challah,
do prayers, share stories and look upward
with gratitude, and when saying good by,
I say, "Later and God bless you."

At this point in my life,
it was and is
worth being called by some,
'a rebel with a cause',
and being misunderstood at times
actually gives me a smile and a chuckle.
Hopefully they, too, will feel
the Presence one day,
and levitate like King David,
so in constant awe.

It never ceases to amaze me,
that my hands don't give up writing again,
the same feeling I had when I wrote
my first book, a sense of excitement,
to challenge myself again
to share my thoughts with you
and all that came down,
especially after I said, "Never again."
One never knows what God has planned for you
and I now learned never to say never
to your God given gift,
your creative mind and hands.
I feel good to now share
the people in my life
that shaped me into who I am now,
at this moment, still wondering
(more then 5 seconds of wondering is a waste for me)
to understand my life,
the world around me...
Something inside seems to talk to me
when I go thru moments of doubt (Satanic forces)
I say out loud, "NOT ON MY WATCH, DUDE."

They are there, known as the negative force,
that's where free choice comes in
and is at times, more often then not,
testing your faith, your whole being to your bowels.
I was spared from slaughter, from being gassed,
I suppose that's why I keep writing
and one must find purpose and meaning
to what you think and put into action.
One thing for sure that relieves my temporary fears,
is that I am somehow reminded...
I still feel I have a purpose, that gives meaning
to the days of my life, till my breath is taken
by the one who inhaled it into me.
(Wow, were did that come from?)

Canter's on Fairfax in Los Angeles is an icon of a deli,
always waiting for us to order the usual.
A bowl of borscht (cold), a boiled potato,
sour cream and bagel chips with butter.
That was Lucy's small portion and mine,
a cup & mucho sour cream.
Lucy was and is so full of abundance,
both spiritually and physically.
She does not think about the extra weight
that a bowel of borscht adds on to the thighs,
and the oversized boiled potato, a few inches more
to the waist and chest (you know what I mean).
We make jokes about the boiled potato
going straight to you know where.
Lucy will be happy me sharing this with you,
as I hope for you all reading this or not,
will get a chuckle visualizing this scene as we do.
Actually we break out in laughter
that heals the heart, you see.

You!

Lucy, my friend, was taken away from her mother,
father, and sisters by the Nazis in 1944 in Hungary.
They arrived in Auschwitz on a cattle car
with hundreds of other children and families,
an unknown journey,
no food, no toilets,
a piece of bread
to last for many days,
to not cause an outbreak.
The Nazis said they were going on a vacation,
and would see many of their friends there.
The Gestapo ordered her to the right
and her mother and father to the left.

For those that don't know the procedure
of Hitler's final solution, massacres
to eradicate the Jewish race...
I feel we must remember
and carry on to ensure 'never again'
and be active to dispel religious
and cultural discrimination.
It could happen to you, your kids,
your grandchildren, your family and friends.
Do not look the other way and
'someone else will take care of it.'
Someone else is you.
I pray the day will come
when the world will see and feel safe.
I think about Lucy more than I realized.
A feeling of sadness overcomes me
when I look at her and visualize her past.
Her pain became my pain,
even though I never shared that with her.
I think she knew when she looked at me,
her eyes full of light and wonder,
and me, squeezing my fingers on my lap
under the table, holding back the tears...

Lucy is so full of courage, determined
to not allow the past to rob her of her dream.
She is 91 years old and it happened 75 years ago.
Does one ever forget the horror, the pain,
the feeling of being helpless
and the world looking the other way.
Maybe the mind cannot fathom
mankind turning against man.
Where were the righteous people living in freedom?
I am 12 years younger than Lucy,
I was spared.
I pray the day will come when
the world will see and feel safe.

Thinking of Lucy. Maybe I'll call her
and hear what's new, always hoping something good,
something positive she will share.
I miss having borscht, with sour cream
and even a boiled potato and my Lucy.
For many years before I met Lucy, she wrote her life story
when the Nazi's took her away from her parents
and put her in a concentration camp.
The story was told thru song, with a 23 member cast.
My friend, the Pink Lady, aka, Jackie Goldberg,
who produces the acclaimed, *Rockin' With the Ages*,
met her in a cafe looking for some singers for the play.
They shared words, and before you knew it
I had a date with Lucy at the iconic deli,
Canter's, on Fairfax in Los Angeles.

It always reminds me of my Papa and me,
buying Challah for Shabbos at Schwartz's bakery
(no relationship... who knows).
When she walked in, I knew it was her.
And she came straight over to me.
Don't need to explain that one,
I feel you get it.
She sat down, and said, "Vat you vant to eat?"
And I said, "Borscht, of course."
It was so long since I had Borscht.
Her eyes said everything that her tongue did not.
Even tho she was jolly, witty and smiled, I felt her pain.
She was very direct and said she wrote
her life story for theatre, commissioned
a renowned director, does not relate to him
and is not having fun.
The kind of fun, when I say fun,
means totally involved, in awe with
what you're doing...hard core fun.

When she said she was not happy with
the renowned director she commissioned,
the idle chatter as usual (in my mind) said Ivor.
Yes, yes, yes,...I called him there and then,
and he took a bus over to Canter's.
Now, know that Ivor is very charming
with his English accent,
smile and light brown skin.
He is from India and raised in England.
They went on and on, and I looked upward
and said, "Thank you God."
He so deserves a break.
And so they met at the Matrix theatre on Melrose,
in Los Angeles and rehearsals started.

I was so happy, beyond happy, and could not stop
looking upward with much thank you's.
Little did I know this would be 8 months of horror,
yet many moments of awe.
Lucy wrote her story that played out on stage very well.
Why did others, including the actors
who were very talented interfere so much
and Ivor perceived as being passive.
Ivor was letting them 'do their thing'
even tho it was scripted.
He believed in them, and I wish they
would have believed in him, as he did in them.
It was beyond painful to watch my friend,
my best friend allowing himself to be so abused.
He took the slaps and never gave up
in spite of nasty, harsh words and actions.

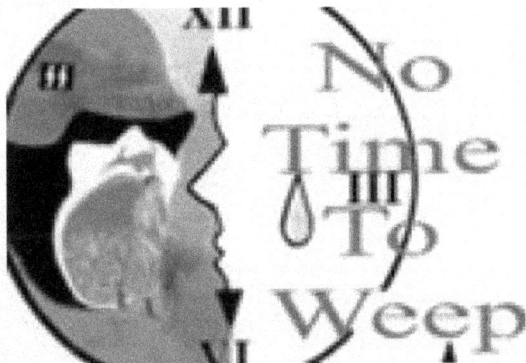

The play was called *No Time To Weep*.
On opening night all the major media came to critique.
It was packed and Lucy, me and Ivor were
so relieved that it came to pass on the stage.
What we were not prepared for was the reviews
of reporters that were unconscious.
Were their eyes closed, were their ears plugged,
did they not see the audience frozen
to their seats in tears and the standing ovation?
Were they blinded by what?
Yet, leave it to God, when the print words
of a major director, producer came
and gave words to Ivor, comparing him
to one of the world's finest directors, Bertold Brecht.
Why could Ivor and Lucy not hang on to that?

Audience member:

COMMENTS

Amazing — the story
the acting
the music & Lyrics
makes hell
& doesn't let go
Very effective &
Simple set
Very moving and
deserves to go on
Well done everyone!

Cyndee Tobin

Ivor sounds depressed, that makes me sad, as I
know what that feels like. I, too, remember my preaching,
"This too shall pass." My Mac computer and I are
surrounded with every kind of self help book, from Hayes,
to Toole, to Joel Osteen, history mavens, pop stars, and
whatever my eyes laid eyes on I bought at Barnes and
Noble, second hand stores and somehow felt their journey,
their words of wisdom. Maybe that thing called osmosis
does work for a while, anyway. Oh yes, then there is
channel flicking. Last night I flicked and flicked from CNN
forward. Finally settled in with a movie of broken relationships
and the ending turning out good.
I never, hardly ever cry, except tears of joy.
I thought about my daughter, Carrie,
that lives in Florida, my princess there
with her wonderful husband
and Dani, Max, Jordan, and the dogs
(when I visit, jump on me as if they had
not seen me in a hundred years)
more than Carrie ever does.
I do get a polite hug from her,
yet I know she loves me mucho.
For Mothers' Day she wrote me,
"To an amazing Mom, who always cares
and never stops loving
with all her being –
Happy Mommy day.
Love Carrie."
It was the word 'Mommy'
that filled my heart and made up
for some of those (yuk times).

Back to Ivor and Lucy.
Called Lucy to have some borscht...
when she does not pick up the phone,
I feel uneasy. I wish I would not
always worry or think the worst.
And why does my brain tell my hand
to pick up the phone and for the hundredth time
my fingers to dial Ivor and Gail,
so I may read the freshly written page
and ask "think it still works."
Ivor always says the same, "Keep writing."
and Gail (can see her lovely smile and chuckle says it all).
But what's with me with this phoneaholic obsession?
Am I that insecure? Maybe it's cause I miss Sam,
my brother, my best friend, my business partner
that did himself in, or maybe I should just write,
like Ivor says, "The only thing that matters
is that you express yourself."

Does this make sense to you,
now that you have digested a bit of this saga,
especially the relationship with Ivor?
Why does he rag on me, like calling
himself a SUCKER (in previous pages)?
Yes, I know his heart, our hearts are dying for spiritual water, food.
Is that so off, to enlist people into the field of dreams,
and play in the sand pits, like kids that are innocent
and in wonderment, pretending we are in the Arabian castles?
And to run with it.
Do I care if people are privately laughing? What happened, Ivor?
Have you forgotten who is really in charge,
and who you work for?
Look into your heart and into the mirror.
I feel sad that you have berated our journey
with its twists and turns, yet so bittersweet, as they say.

Audience member:
COMMENTS

PHENOMINAL!

Penny + Don Feller

Powerful. Intimate.
Inspiring. Thank you
for a beautifully written
produced + acted play / musical
This was one of the
most touching musicals I
have seen in a long, long
time

The *show* is superb
and deeply moving.
Dr. Don Etkes PhD
Dr. Don Etkes PhD

Just a friendly reminder, to myself.
After finishing writing a eulogy letter that turned
into a book, (unbelievable, me not an author) called,
Tears of Stone and my Deal with God,
sold at Barnes and Noble,
I said what I had to say. People tried to encourage
me to write the next chapter (aka, saga)
and I said, "Oh no, enough is enough, never again."
Right, well, look upward and you know who
had something else planned.
I should have remembered never to say never
when it involves God (like everything).
Something inside me would not let me
off the hook, and as usual, asked Ivor to check out
what I wrote, give me feed back, and,
as usual he said, "Keep writing."

As I was glued to the Word document,
I thought, instead of me sending him each page,
maybe, (like a done deal in my mind,)
he would 'coauthor' this part of my life.
I really hoped he would say, "OK."
Courage, believing with all your heart and soul,
steeped in dignity and grace for the wellbeing
for all peoples, is what I wish to always aspire to.
On may 21st, two of my friends, won a political campaign.
One the mayor of Los Angeles, Eric Garcetti,
the times when he sees me, gives me
a meaningful hug and calls me his Cantor.
You can't imagine how that makes me feel,
coming from him, as I have mucho respect for him.
(Those words to make up for all that pain
in the past, in my first book on every other page).

What our elected Mayor does not know yet,
is how I wish to be part of the team, there
on Hill Street (our 'Capitol Hill') Los Angeles,
that I would like to be appointed as Los Angeles'
Ambassador for Goodwill.
Even tho I am not political, tho I suppose one may
call me and Ivor spiritual intellects.
I watched Eric's posture, and very much liked his
grass roots outreach. That is what I, Ivor, and our team
strive to do, reach out to every color
of the rainbow thru our 'political poetic way',
Intertwined in the Music.

My other friend, Nancy Pearlman, running
to be re-elected for trustee for the junior colleges,
a position she has had for many terms
I witnessed in awe - a being that
relentlessly stood on corners of main streets
with her banner waving, with her beautiful smile,
asking to vote for her, long after her few devoted
volunteers went home, her campaign was her
- determination and dancing spirit.
She also, for fun, is a ethnic dancer.
Her opponent had the 'moola', and campaign office.
But he did not have her integrity and spirit,
she kept waving and smiling.
I wonder, when I suggested she look upward
and say thanks all day long, if it helped.
Oh well, she won.
Yaaaaaaaaaaaaaaaaay, Nancy.

Another special person in my life is Gail.
We are, I suppose, total opposites.
She is tall, lovely to look at and totally corporate.
That probably is good for me, as I could never mix
that with what I do. Oh, in case you don't know,
I am a Cantor that reaches out to all people
who have kind of lost their way, temporally lost their faith,
have an empty feeling inside, unconsciously yearning
to reconnect to their roots or be part
of a Universal outreach, to do good deeds
and be kind with your words on your tongue.
Yes, I wear a yarmulka, (kippah) on my head
to remind me daily what I just preached to you
a few sentences above. So I asked Gail if she wanted
to co-write with me and she, like Ivor, probably in cahoots,
said, "Well, let me think about it."
And I thought, thinking is good, until it paralyzes your
creative, God given mind, so now I am waiting
for her and Ivor to live up to their greatness.

One evening, I went to dinner with Gail to celebrate
her finishing her taxes. She always takes care of business,
no matter how difficult her life may be.
She never whines, (like me).
She is my hero in so many ways...
as I am a phonaholic (just made that up).
I call her sometimes, as a joke (more like, oh well,
ask her) to read a page I just wrote.
You see, I am not an author, just sharing my life with you.
Think of it as Gail said 'a lonnng blog'.
P.S. Gail does not have one wrinkle of hardship
in the last year or two; the challenges she had to face
would put me away. Her attitude says it all,
"Tomorrow's another day, be patient."
I have accepted it... this way of thinking
gets one through it all..
I think she should become a rabbi.

I had not heard my daughter's sweet voice
for many weeks. Then, finally when we spoke,
she told me about a young teenage girl who committed suicide.
I gulped, the memories, the pain set in.
It reminded me of my brother Sam, my best friend,
my business partner, my everything.
When the police and mortuary called
and described the suicide...
You see, Carrie, Fabio and the kids live in Florida,
in a small affluent community,
with big affluent homes, cars, etc.
What drives a young soul to do that,
one that has everything one could wish for?
My grandson, Jordan, replied, if only she knew
that this, too, shall pass, it's a temporary feeling.

Twists and turns
One never knows how feelings can change -
an instant thought, an instant feeling,
followed by an ugly goodbye, leaving behind
all to suffer. Be kind, pick up the phone.
I wish I would have known her...

Rozanne...bubbly, high spirited, highly focused
and very informed...our relationship started
with laughter and more laughter and silliness.
She does everything I do not want to be involved with
on a daily basis...Facebook, blogging and Twitter
and makes me look good...
What more can a friend ask for?

Leave it to my loyal publicist Rozanne
to send me a moving picture of our veterans,
with the American flag behind me.
You see I more than love, love America.
When I came over on the Queen Mary in 1948,
with hundreds of child Holocaust refugees,
I saw this most beautiful statue in the water,
pointing her wand at me and saying,
"You are safe, you are in America."...
I was 8 years old. Those words have never left me.
I knew one day I could, would do something
to make those words speak to every nation,
every country, every person that is in bondage.
It was and is my wish for all peoples
to feel safe steeped in their own roots...
In other words, Democracy for all,
regardless of race, religion, culture.
To think our soldiers and all brave hearts
around the world are standing up
to keep their people, their country safe...

My son, David, dropped me off in his classic red,
antique Corvette at my monthly girlfriendship get together.
I always looked forward to getting kind of gussied up
and stepping out of his fancy sports car.
(To get in and out, I had to hold tight to the open door)
as he said, "Mom, can I help you?"
No Cookie, I'm taking my time to make a grand entrance,
you know with that usual flair, in my mind set.
Visualizing the runway into that world of 'red carpet'
I see my friends, (wait! chatter in my head as usual)
"not really friends, Esther, fancy new people
that too, got gussied up to meet other gussied-ups."
I sat across a lady very conservative in black,
fashionable and colorful accessories, a beautiful colorful scarf.
I could feel her vibe...had to be an Argentine.
You see, my daughter is married to an Argentine
and his mother always is dressed with that same vibe. Very lovely.
At the end of the evening, I had no ride home
and asked if anyone can give me a lift home.
Immediately this lady from Argentina said, "Sure, my pleasure."
She never asked, "Where do you live?"
It could have been in Cucamonga.

She is always there for me, when I am not there for myself.
This woman of goodness, truly gives of herself,
never expecting reparation. She has a chain of restaurants
with the most delicious home made empanadas
and always brings me, when in the neighborhood,
my favorite - 'corn' - out of her 36 types,
filled with love, and baked, not fried.
Her blond hair, styled like one of the Ringgold girls
so suits her sparkly blue eyes of compassion and wonderment...
This woman is not a woman of many trivial words,
this woman shows her caring thru her relentless actions
that at times is so needed without asking her for help...
She just intuitively knows...
The only thing is, Argentines drive
as if the road was exclusively paved for them...
I always do a little prayer for her when she drives.

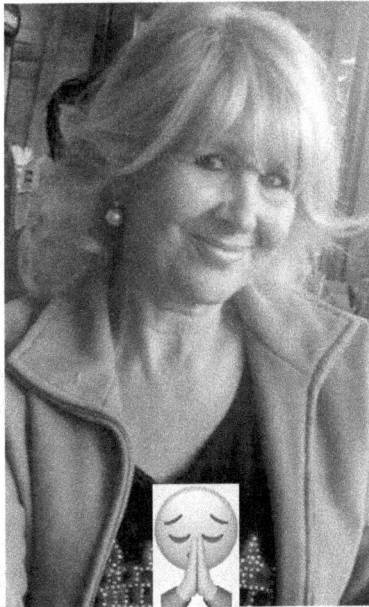

July 20th - 2021 - 10:39
Stella came into our life, (my son and I)
a week ago, and to others on the block
and my friends and family in Florida, and strangers.
Now walking Stella to "pretty please make peepee and poop"
those words of prayer, are supposed to be
of the past, when my kids were born
and grandchildren in diapers.

Stella is a 6 month puppy mix
of Boxer, Pit Bull, Shepherd,
one of God's creation, most sweet...
Stella, the dog my son found in a rescue hotel.
A wonderful, caring place he was guided to
and their eyes met.
You see, my son has a spinal cord condition
that gives him trouble
and has for a year darkened his life.
His life became no life
and my life, was determined to find
an answer to help his condition.
He went to so many recommended doctors,
in the height of the plague aka the Pandemic...

My conversations with God,
morning, noon and night
and in-between
to help him,
to give him comfort,
hope,
something,
you know what I mean.
I hope you never have to witness
one of your children in distress.
And hearing his words,
"What's the use?"
scared me, brought the feelings back
of what happened to my only brother...the suicide.
My brother became my everything
after my Papa went to sit with God
on Shabbos in heaven.

We founded the HOUSE OF CASHMERE STORES
in Beverly Hills
on Brighton Way and Rodeo Drive.
We were one of the 1st stores in the country
that specialized in Cashmere fashions.
We had 13 stores, lived in Malibu,
and with my brother's dark shades,
with that Jack Nicholson smile
and his hair slicked back with (grease handy)
to match his feelings of the day
seemed all is good.
So much more about him in my 1st book...
I wish he had a 'Stella' in his life
for him to feel real love
and affection and healing.
Someone that loves you unconditionally...
that gives you maybe some more self worth,
especially as you care
and take care of something outside of yourself.

Social media was a foreign word for me.
Ivor and I are *old school*,
printing out a most beautiful invitation
and sending it out by *Constant Contact*.
Between Rozanne and us,
physically posting it on trees
in the neighborhood.
Oh yes and putting in an ad
in the *Jewish Journal* and *Beverly Press*
was our way of promoting all our concerts,
High Holy Day services, music meditations,
book signings at *The Grove* in Los Angeles.
And the movie of my life,
a one woman film,
me telling the story
that Ivor produced and directed on a shoe string.

The screenings at the Matrix Theatre told us,
this is the people's choice,
at the end of the movie,
there was silence and sniffing and the clapping,
and that was good enough
and then the plague, aka Corona virus hit.
My granddaughter, Dani, my best friend,
we think alike, even tho I am 79 and she is 21.
We 'Facetime' every day, and never say,
"Goodbye. Later, alligator, after a while, crocodile."
It's our way of saying, "Talk later."
Goodbye is too final for us.
So one morning when visiting from Florida,
she puts the phone in my face
and says, "Saftie, say something to my friends."

I thought we were on 'Facetime' and I said,
"Have courage and be kind."
I got that from the movie Cinderella,
when she looked into the mirror.
Those were the words her mother left her with.
After about 15 minutes,
Dani came into the bathroom,
me trying out a new red lipstick,
(my daily new lipstick schtick)
and with a mucho big smile said,
"You are a super star on TIK-TOK."
Excuse me people, do you know what TIK-TOK is?
Then she said, "You're Grandmawisdom27.
Give the message of the day, every day." For real?

She showed me on her phone
tons of 'likes.'
She said with her soulful
big brown eyes,
"You're in, Saftie. You always have
given a message of hope
and now the world really needs you."
Those words coming from my cool
Dani, that wears short shorts
and tiny tops, with her long
black straight hair covering
her chest that is kind of exposed.
And hangs with a cool in-crowd in
college, I'm over the top,
not sure what that means,
yet I feel it.

I check in with my son and Stella every morning
and say "Hi guys, what's new?."
My son said, "Dropped off Stella at the Dog Spa Hotel
to have a fun day with her new friends."
I looked upward with a smile in my heart.
And they video all day,
so one can see how your baby,
(no matter what age) is doing.

I met a lady at my friend's house for Shabbat.
She was quite interesting
and very into political and world agendas.
She is the opposite of what I am now.
I could relate to her past trials and tribulations
in a big way.
I appreciate who she is now.
Kind of 'been there, done that, still around.
(Ivor put music to my lyrics a song on our album published).
We became buddies.
There was something about her
that drew me to continue our friendship.
She cared to help and did,
thru her immediate response,
especially texting me information
to help my son with his medical condition
and immediately contacting someone that might assist...

What drew me at a distance
was when I told her I am writing
the continuation of the saga of my life,
she said, "Do you use a ghost writer?"
She did read my first book on my life,
as some of you know, I just write.
No edits or re-writes.
The fact that she asked that,
I felt her lack of respect of whom I am
in a deep way, questioning my creativity.
I asked Ivor, "What is a ghost writer?"
I looked up on Google the definition of ghost writer.
'A ghostwriter is hired
to write literary or journalistic works.'
Do I look like someone
that looks to someone else
to express what I feel
and have someone suggest their way of writing.
I am an unorthodox writer.
I just write and am grateful
that my fingers represent
my thoughts and feelings.

After spending many lunches together
and heavy duty talks,
her seeing my ways of being,
I thought of her as a sensitive being.
Her question took me by surprise
and kind of hurt.
I felt insulted and not recognized
for the gift God gave me,
to just be me, expressing myself
thru music, poetry, prose
and recently authoring 5 books
thru the arts
all on my own, my own style.
Thank God I have overcome.
I appreciate me and feel my worth.
I think the fact that she was born in Israel
made me feel closer to being in Israel...

So I wake up in the morning,
the lyrics of *Come Up for the Rising*
by Bruce Springsteen,
ringing in my ears.
A song I recorded for the album,
Songs Of The Prophets
with Ivor, singing in duet.
I so want to feel that again.
Come on up for the rising.

It's Friday, almost Shabbos time...
IT'S A SIGN!!
Come on up for the rising on Shabbos,
I want to feel your hands in mine,
tonight, tonight on Shabbos.
Yes. Tonight is Shabbat...
the 4th Commandment:
'Honor Thy Sabbath'
for me this is a sign,
as I did not realize when using his lyrics,
the last line, "Come on up for the rising tonight..."
Feeling this on Friday and my precious Shabbat
is almost here tonight as the sun sets...

So what does this all mean?
People in your life, that just come and go?
Or does one tolerate and try to understand
and forgive when one feels misunderstood
and not appreciated for your worth?
Down the street from my building is a salon,
a hair salon that draws rockers,
anyone and everyone that is cool,
or dreams to be cool and unique.
What I mean by that is no one does hair extensions,
dreadlocks, color like a mermaid and understands,
no matter how far out, to some.
(Who cares?)
In fact when one has their hair done at this salon,
be prepared to give a 'bad ass' smile to the paparazzi...

The girl who created this salon, a piece of art,
is wise and really cares about people's emotions.
She too, has been there, done that
and is still around.
Her understanding of hair is beyond
what you learn in hair school.
Hair has a spirit and let's you know
when it is unhappy and needs some lovin' care.
She gets it. She has the fix.
Then there is a young dude who is so gifted,
if only he would believe in himself like we do.
Then there is another beautiful being,
dresses like a Picasso painting
and his cut and colors in his curly hair,
slightly parted on the side is a show stopper.
Their personalities and characters match their hearts.
They know what it is like to be different
and thru perhaps words that hurt.

That makes them so very special.
Special enough for me to want
to hang with them,
especially when I'm feeling displaced
and out of my skin,
they and the owner bring me back...

I live down the street and get some hugs
whenever they are there.
Also about my hair schtick,
I play with my bangs with one day,
lavender with a mix of green high lights.
When I get the yucky feelings and my spirit says,
"It's the hair, Cookie. The bangs don't like
the yellow and orange highlights."
I go 300 hundred feet down the block.
Walk in and get a greeting, "OK, we have a half hour,
before one of our rockers comes in."
(You see, I hardly ever make an appointment)
No, I'm not a diva or queen bee, or maybe
a little spoiled by my precious friends
who understand my spiritual obsession with my hair.
I walk out after a half hour and throw
a billion kisses upward in gratitude
for my friends that 'get it.'
They are above anything petty.

At times, all I ask for is to bring me back
to the moments that gave me joy.
You know one moment, one pure moment
can feel like a lifetime...
then on to the next precious moment,
and next and next and then what?
God always gets me out of my funk.
As I'm writing, I see out the window
my son and Stella, the diva,
are coming back from a walk.
Actually they looked like they just got off a plane.
He is wearing one of those cool cowboy hats
like the country singer, Blake Shelton,
performing with his girl friend for the Grammys in Nashville.
And the diva, Stella, a scarf around her neck.
Wow, thank you, God.
My son is talking to a cute girl walking her dog.
I have not seen him so animated in years.
I wish he would charm her with his hidden talent.
If you heard him sing and accompany himself
on the keyboard, you would go 'meow'
and would track him down.

Meet my dear friend, Destiny.
A killer smile and twinkle in her eyes.
It was High Holy Days.
In walks a handsome family,
dressed like something out of the Godfather movie.
Their presence reeked with humility,
yet that look on their faces,
you felt like when you see Marlon Brando
hand over the throne to Michael, his son.
After the services, they introduced themselves.
I asked them, "Where did you hear about our services?"
Her father said that his daughter, Destiny,
is Catholic and Italian and wants to become Jewish.
He found my ad in the local paper.
I was at a loss for words.
An Italian Catholic family raised in the church,
baptized, felt something more being here,
coming to a synagogue,
listening to my words and chanting.

He understood his daughter, Destiny's feeling
of the presence of God that reaches
the bowels of the soul and converting
to Judaism, to be part of the tribe.
Destiny was wearing a small
silver Jewish star around her neck for many years.
Destiny now was promoting Shabbat at Lenny's Deli,
in the back room, which you know
was dedicated to us, Shabbos Buddies.
She actually drove around on Fridays, meeting people,
and saying, "Hey, come for Shabbos, I'll drive you there."
She said to me, "Let's rent a van and pick people up."
I will never, ever forget one Shabbos,
when 10 little girls in their teens walked in
with small bouquets of white flowers
and handed them to me
and they asked me to bless them.
I had a flash back of me being hidden
in the church, running from the Nazis.

Now Destiny comes into my life.
Now, reminiscing, it was a sign,
people come into your life for a reason
and maybe it's best not to question,
it reveals its purpose as we stride forward
with some wisdom unexpected.
Destiny moved to Florida, went back to collage,
studying literature, becoming a respected, renown poet.
I sure miss having hot chocolate milk with her
at the Peninsula Hotel in Beverly Hills, LOL.

I would now like to discuss
a universal theme...Constipation.
I would not have brought this up,
but my son came in while I was writing
and said Stella had a funny poop.
That's all I needed to hear. It reminded me
when my kids were born,
if their bowel movement looked funny color.
Yes, got concerned. Being a para-chaplain,
volunteering at a hospital,
visiting patients to chant a singing blessing,
seeing all the tubes in their bodies
always made me so sad
and at the same time so grateful,
immediately thanking God
that I was, most of the time, regular.

Early in the morning I texted my son, "Anything?"
He replied, "She pooped."
The queen bee-diva is today getting a tan,
having a manicure and chilling out with her friends.
While my son is working his ass off
and me keeping you posted.
Of course I also Tik-Tokked this saga on Tik-Tok
and they commented, "YAY"
and some, believe it or not, "Mazel tov" (congratulations).
P.S. please, listen to your body.
Get informed what foods your body is craving,
your organs are talking to you.

Me take a break now, it's Sunday.
I'm going outside, look around and say to myself,
"Where can I have more fun, just chill out
and sort of be mindless, just be?"
After all that tension, but a good ending – she pooped.
The wind blew me in the direction of *The Grove*,
an outdoor international, designer shops and Nordstrom
and Groundworks Organic Coffee.
Yeah. I stopped at my favorite place for some fruit
and strolled to Nordstrom.

They have a very nice ladies' room,
with a powder room and a changing table
for mommies and babies.
I washed my nectarine, white nectarines are so sweet,
I'm such a creature of habit,
always buying the same fruits and same routine.
I sat in this beautiful gray oversized velvet arm chair.
A feeling I'm in a luxurious hotel and oh, let's say in Paris.
I was about to take a bite from this juicy nectarine.
A lady walks in with a baby crying in her arms.
She tried to sooth the baby and said, "It's OK. It's OK.
It's just poop, darling. Mommie will change you."

I sat there and was not sure if I was dreaming,
after all that was an experience with Stella and poop.
I do have delayed reactions.
This is getting to be too melodramatic.
Then another woman walked in and they said, "Hi,"
to each other. With the baby screaming,
her friend asked her, "What's wrong?"
Diarrhea.

I'm out of here, coffee time.
Next to Nordstrom, Groundworks.
I ordered my usual, took a zip,
sat down outside and the same two women
came out and sat at the table
next to me and smiled.
The babies started to cry.
Look, I love babies.
I wanted to have another baby.
I was in my 30s, even when I was pushing 40s.
I was waiting for my true love
on a shining white horse
to sweep me off my feet.
I'm getting melancholic.
I can't even drink this coffee, the color.

You know, I feel like Stella is my baby.
She is my son's dog that I wished for him.
I bought her, at CVS this morning,
the cutest white dog for dogs to play with.
I was so looking forward to seeing her,
after my son would pick her up
from the spa hotel when he finished work.
I thought he would bring her in to say, 'Hi.'
You see, my son lives in our building next door.
I am trying very hard to give him his space.
Ever since his spinal condition
and what that could lead to, I worry.

Now with Stella in his life,
I know it's not a girlfriend in his life,
hopefully that too, shall appear.
But I just wanted to hug her
and give her the furry white dog
and say, "Sleep tight."
I called Ivor with a lump in my throat
and he said, "Let him be."
It hurts sometimes when you love so much,
when you care so much,
when you want to fix everything,
so that I can sleep thru the night.
Maybe it's me that needs some attention,
professional, I mean.
Ivor does not understand.
He has no children or a dog.

TAKING A BREAK...

So much has come up and down
since I've had the inspiration to continue this saga.
A woman that I hung out with at times
to share a meal or chat over a cup of coffee,
became a huge disappointment to my being.
It was like being with Jeckyll and Hyde.
One misinterpreted word turned into words at me,
that made me wonder why am I in her company.
She texted me that she and her friends
thought my skin looked like lizard skin,
that I am evil at times and look like 190 years old.
What's with you, girl?
I choose not to run every 2 minutes
for injections in my face,
or send 'selfies' of my body and face to match.
I overlooked these virtues in her.
I felt underneath all that skin
and body plumped up was, a little girl,
unsure of herself thru her hurtful past
and that is what I related to, as I've been there...

As I suppose at this point, and from my 1st book,
that I am a child Holocaust survivor.
Being raised in convents on the run,
from our hiding space in the church,
I heard the most beautiful music and voices singing.
I felt safe, I know I was with God.
And that feeling of wanting to be close
to the music never went away.

Coming to America, I was so excited and so scared
to open my mouth to sing at a recital.
A croak sound came out,
and I ran out and never came back, until now.
I really had to search so hard for my existence.
And the people in my life.
My family, my Ivor, my friends at Sirens Salon
where I have my bangs colored in pop colors
according to my spirit of the day.
And my baby, Stella, my dog.
I'M DONE with people that come
into my life with an evil eye...
in spite of it all, I still believe people are good at heart,
words written by Anna Frank,
as they were born pure,
then life takes over.

I was just thinking,
having the guts,
the something that drives you
to say what you feel, think, project onto paper.
Words and language you probably would not
say out loud or directly to that person's face
or your true opinion in a tense situation,
especially about politics.
Divorces and murders can come
from political differences.
What's so cool,
when your fingers take over on the computer,
it has no boundaries, no ghost writers,
no edits or rewrites.
Only what YOU choose to say or do…
It's one of the best self understanding
of what happened in the past till now.
It's as you're reliving your life
and examining what you did
and others did to you
and commenting in 'real time'…

So, if you want to clear up some things of the past,
and be clearly heard,
start writing and you got your chance
and will never feel *should have, could have...*
P.S. or sign up on TIK TOK.
Just imagine getting up in the morning
or middle of the night
with a feeling or thought,
then and there,
in that minute,
millions of people view your posting...
It works, 'instant therapy.'
You could send the money you saved
to your favorite charity,
something like that,
you know what I mean.

Back to the recital…
That's why I asked Ivor if he would do with me in duet,
a recital I never had.
In my first book,
Tears Of Stone and My Deal With God,
I expressed my fears.
To sing in front of people,
always remembering the croak
that came out of my throat.
Now the recital is scheduled for August 29th, 2021.

If you were a fly on the wall
and witnessed the uncontrollable emotions
between Ivor and my 10 year accompanist
and friend where 2 times a week,
(how blessed I am) down the street worked my voice,
especially with 'Ava Maria.'
When I uttered the words in Latin, as I sung it,
it took me back hiding and listening
to the nuns singing on the alter,
where I wanted to be,
closer to God.

It's hard for me to find the words
that describe the outburst from Ivor
that did not match anything I said or did.
I just asked him to rehearse with me
next to me, like a duet.
He sat in the chair across the room, like a judge,
like back in the days when the croak came out of my throat.
This is crazy, Ivor loves my voice,
that's why he sings with me
and harmonizing to each breath I don't take.
We sound so beautiful together.
He is a rock singer and I am a Cantor
who sings liturgical music...
It is Ivor that encouraged me
to use my lower range
and could sound like a country singer
by approaching them like prayers.
I always wanted to sing those pop songs.
And he coached me and here we are
so ready and all this 'yuk' of shouting,
like out of a horror movie.

Ivor and my accompanist were at odds
right from the beginning.
Before COVID, AKA the plague
we were invited to perform
for major events, in large venues.
Ivor created a music score to every song to die for.
It caught the attention of many hearts around the world.
The track became our accompanist, our orchestra.
It worked. Ivor made it happen thru his gifted ear.
My accompanist knew nothing about Ivor's creativity
and Ivor knew nothing about my accompanist's
background of degrees in music,
especially classical and pop and touring with major bands.
My accompanist was horrified.
Out of our friendship and commitment to the project,
he would continue and then never again.

I was heart broken in a way,
as I liked how he accompanied me,
very simple, no background track,
almost like being at Juliard Music Academy.
Oh well, "Dream big Esther",
from Tut, daily messages from the universe.
Now as I'm reminiscing what happened a week ago
and now, a week later,
how sweet everything sounds,
as if it never happened,
that 'Yuk' the satanic forces gave in
to the beautiful God given sounds of music.
The fly on the wall disappeared.

The recital I never had is almost here.
This Sunday, Aug 29, 2021 at 3:30pm.
Already I'm not sleeping well,
waking up with doubts.
I so want to be the best I can with my singing voice.
Another chance for me to really,
really produce those clean,
gentle sounds with conviction,
always with a gentle vibe.
That is what my Cantor Alan Michelson taught me.
All in my 1st book.
Too tired to explain it again,
the whole saga about my fear of the croak coming out,
especially the starting note of Ava Maria.
Yet there is a part of me that says, "It's OK, you're covered."
Your Cantor in heaven is smiling down
and saying, "Gentle, don't push."
I took all the extensions out of my hair,
and highlighted a pale aqua.
It makes me feel more calm.
Color really matters, it affects your psyche.

Hi, Tuesday, August 31, 2021, 10:34pm.
I'm back…So much to share with you.
I'm all over the place in my head,
where to start or finish, done…
Not yet, Esther.
The little girl, Esther, 10 years old
that auditioned for the recital,
and that croak that came out of her throat and ran away.
Now 69 years later, looking,
feeling the feelings like yesterday,
(people say get over it)
am proud of me now,
able to share with you, "I'M OVER IT."

When the music sound of Ava Maria started.
Flashes of me in the church,
hiding behind the pews when on the run,
and then I saw God smiling and saying,
"You're covered, Esther, go for it.
Be gentle to Esther and Ava Maria,
sing it like a prayer."
I looked at the few people sitting in total silence,
smiling at me and giving me the 'high sign.'
people I barely knew.
And Ivor next to me,
all he endured all these years of my 'saga,'
who always said, "Get over it."
Watch and hear this, Ivor.
I slowly parted my lips,
and Ivor, God bless him,
harmonized to give support, and I DID IT.
Yes, my friends and all those that never even knew
I sang the prayers, songs out of the cantorial liturgy,
now I sang in Latin and Italian.
Know this, I tell you,
I wish for you all to have an Ivor to believe in you,
thru thick and thin, as some say.

A few weeks ago I met two young girls,
my granddaughter, Dani's age,
in their early twenties at a café, having coffee.
I can't remember how we got into a conversation,
maybe a comment on my aqua hair that gives me calm.
In a lovely British accent, with beautiful blue eyes,
no fake lashes, natural blond long hair,
she smiled and we got into a magical conversation.
She expressed her love of the harp she plays,
especially the prayer, 'Ave Maria.'
Of course, leave it to God, in Divine time,
to fulfill one of my wishes.
The instrument I always hoped for, a harp,
to accompany me with 'Ave Maria.'
It's a 'done deal' I said, and she agreed.
Her friend, her roommate, so beautiful,
so endearingly, so patient,
took in this intense talk of music…
And they live down the street from me.
I invited them to the recital.

They came and sat in the front
on a uncomfortable chair and smiled at me.
It was like a rainbow over their beings.
A light shinned on their faces, is all I saw.
The girl that plays the harp
uttered the words of one of the poems I recited,
'The Road Less Traveled' at the end of the recital.
At that very second, the light over their faces vanished,
and real time set in with 'high signs'
and clapping, and so much true love
of what they all experienced.
I think, one does not keep clapping and teary eyed
and throwing kisses my way, our way,
me and Ivor, surely, must have experienced something.
Ivor thinks the two girls,
are angels sent to us…
Yes, "Done."
I can't or want to explain any further,
just leave it alone Esther, and do your usual,
"Look upward and say Thank you, God."

Sept 22 Wed 2021…
So much to share again, this ongoing saga of mine.
Then again, Estherleon, something inside is so grateful
that my fingers are still full of pep.
I feel my brain, my heart are talking to each other,
saying, "Just type, girl."
Just finished officiating HIGH HOLY DAYS…
I feel I did a good job. I am grateful
that God lifted my voice to the heavens,
especially when I had enough nerve
to do the prayer, 'Kol Nidre,' a cappella.
In my first book and now a movie,
I had the opportunity, because of Ivor,
you know, who brings dust to life on a shoe string,
to share my life on screen.

I think I have already shared this saga,
about always wanting to feel close to the music
that made me feel so safe being hidden in the churches
on the run from the Nazi's...
Coming to America, a shy kid of 9 years old
was not very welcomed by other kids,
especially in school.
This was in 1948.
God bless the kids in this generation
that not only welcome immigrants,
the kids of today have such pure hearts,
not afraid to express their feelings,
the pain of others and go into action,
trying to help in so many creative ways.
Anyhow, when I tried out for an audition,
only a 'croak' came out, and everyone,
the kids in the audience laughed,
and I ran into the bathroom
and cried and never came back.
More of that in my first book...

Now I think...
The first time in my life, especially after the recital,
and from the positive response, I feel a divine power in me,
(maybe it's the blue, lavender hair)
or maybe it's about Freddy Mercury,
from Bohemian Rhapsody...and relating,
dealing with my brother's suicide and me now.
The melody and lyrics that haunt me enough
to want to share this with you, as I dare to perform this live.
The vision of Freddy Mercury coming out on stage,
smiling and strutting to the piano,
thousands of people clapping as they knew
as he played the first chord.
In so many ways the lyrics 'Mama' in the song,
is my brother's relationship with my mother,
prophetically talking of his own end,
and how it's time to throw it all away.
And it would make her cry with the regrets
of no changing the outcome with no tomorrow.
Accepting the final outcome with no tomorrow,
and really after the intention to do what he wanted to do,
made it not matter 'really' to anybody, but Mama and me.
Time to go, leaving every one... to regret what they did.
Knowing the actions he is taking,
actions he does not want to take,
and wishing he had never been born,
leading him to the new world of acceptance
where he would not be judged.

At times, we can become so vulnerable
like my brother, Sam.
So easy to get lost in darkness
in your head and heart.
When you're not truly connected
with some special person to turn to,
bottom line... God, your refuge...
When you allow the negative force to kick in,
and that satanic force smiles,
it's the demons that have to be exorcized,
that thrive on your blood and guts.
Maybe for some, it feels like the only way
out of this relentless, ugly inner torture,
is to cause pain to others and justify it
by wishing you were never born and someone must die.
And in the lyrics. who is the one we share this with – 'Mama.'
Too sad... In the end it really mattered to me
because I have been suffering with his passing all these years.

So I will bravely share this live, on stage
and that vision of Freddy Mercury
singing those lyrics,
my interpretation of those lyrics,
wishing I would have known
what my brother Sam was feeling
and did not share, and did himself in.
Sparing 'Mama' the truth, by family and friends
saying that he was in a fatal car crash.
A mother knows the truth...

My heart is heavy with all that I just wrote.
If only Sam and others out there had buddies like I have,
at a Rocker Hair Salon,
a few steps up the block from my building I live in.
I think I wrote this before, here I go again.
When I get up in the morning,
I throw on my oversized coat,
dark shades and cap to walk one hundred feet
to get my Starbucks pour-over coffee
with steamed half and half thru the alley.
I usually peek in the Rocker Salon, *Sirens*,
to make sure all is OK, even tho its gated,
and I greet the same homeless people
in the alley, their home.
They smile and I do the usual,
throw up my arms
towards the heavens and sing, 'Hallelujah'
and they smile and say, "Amen."

A beautiful, insightful female
owns the soulful, colorful, hair salon,
Sirens in West Hollywood.
One day, we made a deal
after she highlighted for the millionth time my hair,
a different pop color, according
to my inner color mood of the day.
I said, "How much I owe you?"
And she said, "0" and I said, "No way,"
and then we made the deal: I paid her
and she gave this to those homeless in the alley,
on her way to Starbucks.
A 'Hi' or smile is all they,
the homeless in the alley, wished for.
I wish for you all to have a friend,
a buddie like this woman, with baby pink hair,
a heart the reeks with wisdom and compassion.
I wish a friend like this blessed soul…
onto you, in this life.

I hope you will get to know
and understand Ivor
more in my 1st book,
Tears Of Stone and My Deal With God.
Still waiting for Ivor to say a few words
before this goes to print.

I feel now I want to say,
no point going on and on.
I said what I had to say…
Look upward morning,
noon and night
and in-between.

Stick with God
and you will never feel alone.
Ponder and pray at least 3 times a day.

P.S. To Carrie and David, my children I gave birth to,
I always wanted children, wanted to be a mommy
from a very young age. I got my wish...
And then was blessed with Max, Jordan, Dani and Mikey,
my grandchildren; and Stella, Daisy, Kali and Emma,
our dogs. And thank you Fabio for taking such good care
of my daughter and grandchildren.
And thank you, all my beautiful friends
for including me in your lives.

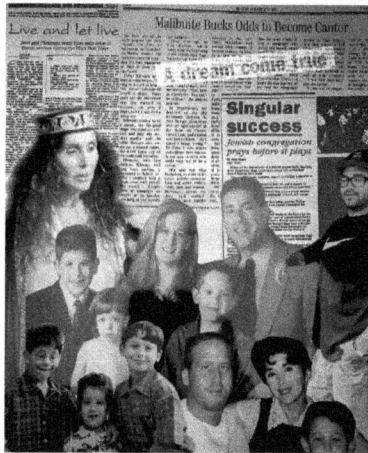

Carry on, Carry on.
And...Thank you, God, for your presence
every moment of the day that made me feel
I am not alone in those moments of despair and sadness,
made me feel, as if you were saying,
"It's OK, let me take over. Just rest"
Thank you for giving me the courage and the joy
to play with life in all the creative mediums...
My life was and is lived with purpose and meaning,
my life was and still is lived in wonderment and awe
Never say goodbye. I say, "Later."

I wish to thank all those devoted folks
that gave me the 'high sign,' no worries…
Michael Rosen, Lionel Ochoa,
Michael at the Beverly Press,
and all those in heaven, doing Shabbos with God,
always giving me a sign to feel 'you're covered.'

As I always light a candle for my Papa, my Mother,
my brother, Sam, and Mikey, my grandson,
"Keep sending your signs to your Dad,"
and Philsie, Kelly, Renée, Laura, Irving,
Cantor Alan Michelson - your voice,
Rabbi Levi Meir - your wisdom,
Aunt Dore, Uncle Alex, Roxanne,
Lisa and Uncle Michel,
Aunt Sonja and Aunt Dina,
Linda, Daniel, and my Ajna,
unconditional caring and patience,
and Mona for taking care of you know who…
if I forgot anyone, forgive me. -e

Epilogue...

Writing all this has helped me understand
what I tried to forget and others kept saying, "Move on, girl."
Well, I understand those well meant, kind words of caring...
But how can one dismiss
all that has haunted you all your years,
all that kept you from really moving on
to be your best and feel your worth...
Hallelujah, 'got the blessing,' as some say.
I like that, because those that say that,
have really suffered and worked their being,
their soul, in such faith and wanting to believe,
and taking the steps in faith with such support,
on earth and from above...
That's the bottom line for me,
some say 'a rebel with a cause.'
I'll take...another chance at life
to sing away unto the heavens
until my last breath. -e

BE...what you want to be remembered as
(write your own eulogy...(LOL)

Estherleon and Ivor Pyres

Lyric book

The Devine Gypsies

He, Ivor, in the last hour, came thru
and presented me our life together...
DIVINE GYPSIES

THINKING OF YOU – Ivor Pyres

Life can be meaningful - Life can be precious
Life can take you anywhere you want to go
Life could be your window to the world
Where all you see is your destiny

Life could be precious - Life could be honorable
If you don't burn the bridges to you Life can be precious
Life can be awesome Go Live for today and live

I'm thinking of you I'm thinking of you
I'm thinking of you I'm thinking of you

There's all these treasures in your soul
There's always something that's good to behold
And all that is coming into play for you
Life can be beautiful a bed to lie in
Life could be a thorn of weeds
Life could be a miserable experience
Or it could be a jewel to cherish

I'm thinking of you I'm thinking of you
I'm thinking of you I'm thinking of you

Life can be precious
Life has it's own way of dealing with things
Life could be yours what's yours is another's choice
Mine is my choice mine has my meaning
Mine is the devil and angel questioning my reason
Mine is the motion burnt on the tongues of my life
My is the differences set for my days
Mine is the one and only experience
That I share with no one

I'm thinking of you
I'm thinking of you
I'm thinking of you
I'm thinking of you

BRAND NEW DAY – Ivor Pyres/Estherleon

There's a brand new day
On the horizon today
There's a dream coming into view
Coming into view

There's a sheltering storm
That's under the sky
There's a dream
Coming into view
There's a road there's a fire
There's a certain desire.

There's a dream on the horizon

There's a life that shines
Showing the way
There's a world
That will never be the same

There's a road there's a fire
There's a certain desire.

There's a dream on the horizon
Brand new day

WHAT IF   *Estherleon & Ivor Pyres*

What if the world stood still for one day
For peace and humanity
Would find it's way
You and me can be a force
So that there will be no remorse
For the children's sake
Shout out loud and forever say
Enough, Enough
No more hunger no more wars
Let's make peace no matter what it takes
For goodness sakes

And if just for one more day
All the world would still stand up and say
We will find another way
And the world stood still
And made it's way
Enough, Enough
No more hunger no more wars
Let's make peace
No matter what it takes
For goodness sakes for humanity's sake
Still believing in that special day

Images of
Estherleon
as drawn by
student
"Buddy"
in England

WHO AM I – Estherleon/Ivor Pyres

Who am I if only I
Who am I if only me

I'm alone
No one else
To give me breath
To know I'm me

So I reach out to you,
Hold my hand
Let me walk with you
Through this life
Be my light be my hope
Set me free to know

Now I am now I'm me
Now I'm whole,
Now I'm free
You're my light, a reflection
Of the me I'm meant to be

So I look
To my faith in you
I will walk
Through this life
Be my light be my hope
Set me free to know
Who I am

IN A HEARTBEAT - Estherleon/Ivor Pyres

In a heartbeat I'll be there
Cause you're my sweet angel
I've been looking everywhere
Cause you're my sweet angel
At times when you're feeling so insane
And can hardly bare the pain

In a heartbeat I'll be there
You're my sweet Angel
My wings of strength will shelter you
Cause you're my sweet angel
Your life in my life I promise you

In a heartbeat I'll be there
To hold your hand and walk with you
My sweet Angel I just really care
You can trust it I know it's rare

You're my sweet angel
Of goodness that I found
That is what turned my heart
And my life around

So in a heartbeat I'll be there
To give my sweet Angel
All the love and care

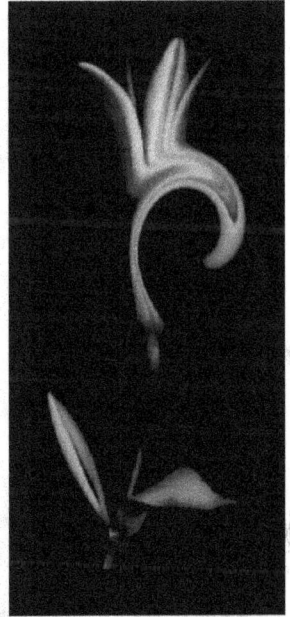

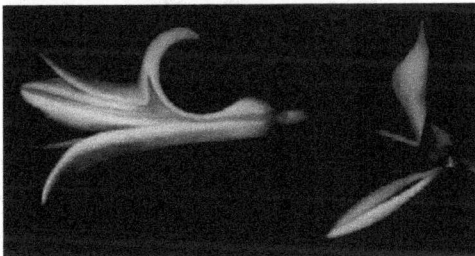

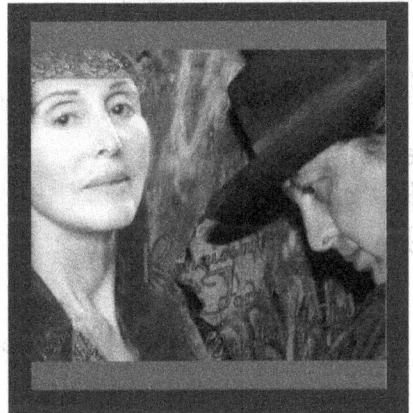

ASK YOUR HEART – *Estherleon / Ivor Pyres*

Ask your heart

Ask your heart

Ask your heart

Ask your heart

Ask your heart

Ask your heart where you belong (ask your heart)

A singular voice or a harmonious song

A shape in the distance

Or a mountain so tall (ask your heart)

A benefit to mankind or a singular call

A voice that's in the winds of change

Or a wind that destroys every plain

Ask your heart where you belong   (ask your heart)

A singular voice or a harmonious song

Harmony harmony   (ask your heart)

Singular voices in love

Harmony harmony (ask your heart)

Singular voices as one

One heart one voice one love one self one world

(Ask your heart)

Harmony harmony (ask your heart)

Singular voices in the distance waiting to be heard

A beautiful song the whistle of a bird

Ask your heart

The roar of a lion the silence of a butterfly

Harmony harmony   (ask your heart)

A baby's first voice my oh my

Singular voices are we singular people we shouldn't be

All together now in harmony

Harmony harmony

Singular voices in love singular voices as one

One voice one heart one love one self one world

Ask your heart

Harmony harmony harmony harmony

Singular voices in the distance

Singular voices in love

Singular voices as one

Ask your heart

One voice one heart one self one world

Ask your heart

Harmony harmony harmony harmony

Voices as one

AMAZING WOMAN   Estherleon/Ivor Pyres

I celebrate my laugh lines on my face
Having lived a great life I did not waste.
Day by day I learned to play the game of life
in it's magic way Been there done that still a round

I'm an amazing woman that searched and found
A truth in life for me so profound.
I'm an amazing woman in every way
With a deeper understanding in space and time.
A sacred space that's yours and mine
-

No wannabe's for me I took action and kept my faith
Always believing I found my faith.
The journey started long ago
On Life's terms I gave it all no regrets I felt it all
Been there done that still a round

I'm an amazing woman that searched and found
A truth in life for me so profound.
I'm an amazing woman in every way
With a deeper understanding in space and time.
A sacred space that's yours and mine
A sacred space that's yours and mine
Been there done that
Been there done that still around
-

A truth in life for me so profound.
I'm an amazing woman in every way
With a deeper understanding in space and time.
A sacred space that's yours and mine
A sacred space that's yours and mine

CONSTANTLY – Ivor Pyres

How constantly your feelings shape my world
How constantly I think of you and then
How constantly I give myself time
Waiting for you to stand in line with me

How constantly I try to shape my world
Round your idea of my destiny
How constantly you take my time
How constantly you give me pleasure.
How constantly you take me back
How constantly you bring me back
How constantly I'm thinking of being with you
And you and you

Will buy me hope for the present and the future
Will buy me hope forever if I try
I'm going to be with you for now and forever
Will you buy your time with me

IF ONLY - *Estherleon/Ivor Pyres*

If only I knew you were feeling so blue

I'd have been there in a heartbeat for you

If only I knew the pain you were in

I would have been there in a whim.

I'd put on in my wings soar through the sky

Didn't know why you wanted to die

You wanted to die and now I cry

That you didn't share

What does it take to feel that way

A disappointment that never would go away

A love affair that didn't fair

A discussion that you didn't share

A tormented you that nobody knew

But I am me a big part of you

EXCEPTIONAL MERIT

For Original Song
"If Only"
composers: Estherleon &Ivor Pyres
for film: Estherleon: Tears of Stone

WRPN Women's International Film Festival

2019

That you didn't share That you didn't share

That you didn't share That you didn't share

That you didn't share That you didn't share

I am me a big part of you

That you didn't share That you didn't share

That you didn't share That you didn't share

That you didn't share I am me a big part of you

A tormented you that nobody knew

But I am me a big part of you

If only I knew that you're ok

Perhaps some of that pain would go away

It wasn't fair to leave that way

To leave me in pain each

moment of the day

I am me a big part of you

If only I knew in your own way

spirits are connected

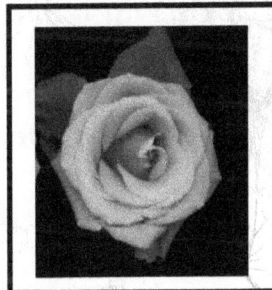

13

WHEN   Estherleon/Ivor Pyres

When -When will you come back
When -You've been goon so Long
When -Will you let me know
When -We're no longer apart

When -You'll come back to me when I need you
When -I know that I can do without you
When -Will I know that you will see
When -ahhhhhhhhhhh
When when when when

When -Will I see your Face again
When -Will you come home again
When -Will you be there for me
When -I will take you for a ride
On a ship that no one else can sail
When -When do you promise me
When -Will it be
When -Will it be you tell me
When -Will it be

Ahhhhhhhhhhhhh ahhhhhh
When when when when

When -When will you come home
When -I'm coming home

When -When will you come home
When -I'm coming home

When

14

YOU ARE MY EVERYTHING – Estherleon/Ivor Pyres

Just knowing you're just a touch away
Just knowing you're in the next room
Just a breath away
Keeps me feeling safe in that special way.

To Know and to feel
Your touch in such a way
Keeps my Sunday blues away.
To feel and know
We're still a team
On each other's side,
Fills me with love and pride
Fills me with love and pride

Having made it
Through the lows and highs
I feel so grateful to feel this life
I wish this for everyone
That's on my path
From the early morning dew
Till the sunset sets
On the rainbows hew.

I wish this for everyone
When all is said and done
You'll still be my everything
And we'll have won
Just knowing you're just a touch away
Keeps me feeling strong from day to day.

You are my everything you are my everything

15

FEED THE CHILDREN – Ivor Pyres

When children are born
Life takes over
They open their eyes to a new reality
Their cry is the first sound from their mouth
Their first few years decides their future

So feed them life
Feed them hope
Feed them the glory of being alive
Hold their hands hold them close
Give them their place on this earth

Their eyes call out for you to guide them
Their words are peace their hearts are open
You can't take their love away

Thank you
"Buddy"
in England

So feed them life
Feed them hope
Feed them the glory of being alive
Hold their hands hold them close
Give them their place on this earth

Chorus
Feed them life
Feed them love
Feed them the glory of being alive
Hold their hands hold them close
Give them their place on this earth

ALL IN ALL – Estherleon / Ivor Pyres

The rainbows fell on you
The light fell on me
The days are never over
They are mine

Life cries out for your sound
The dreams I first lost
The love that I shared with you
The world is mine

The light surround you and me
The days are sent to you
The moon stood still for you
The Lights they set on you
All in all all all in all
I see a future

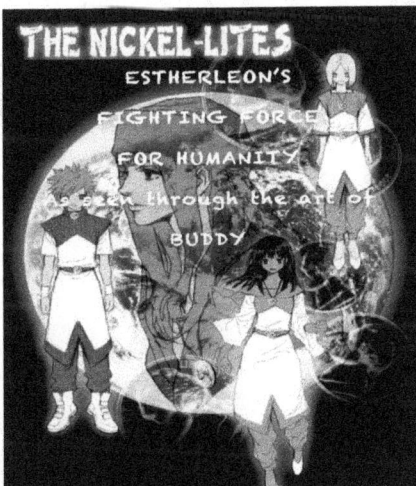

The rainbows fell on you
The lights fell on me
The days are never over
They are mine

All in all all all in all I see a future

SAY YES SAY NO – Estherleon/Ivor Pyres

Say yes say yes

Say to everything but only if it feels so right

Say yes to everything take a chance and ride the tide

Say yes to chance I'll take my chance

Say yes - say no when you gut rebels

Say no trust your insides it can tell trust trust you

Don't be afraid you really know when its yes or no

Listen to your beat dance to your beat sing to your beat

Your insides know yes can be no and no can be yes

Seek your own truth

Dig deep inside life will be come just a joyous ride

Say yes to whatever comes your way

Take a chance don't run away go for it all the way

Say yes to what ever come your way

Take a chance don't run away go for it all the way

Sing a song do a dance play it play it out

Like romance it's the game of life

Take a chance say yes say yes

Say yes and take that chance do it do it

Say yes and take a chance

Say yes say yes and take a chance

Play it out like romance

Take a chance everything

Say yes say yes say no say yes trust in you

When it yes or no listen hey listen to your beat

Hey dance to your beat whoo!!! sing to your beat

Your insides know yes can be no

Play it out like romance

It's the game of life take a chance

Seak your own truth take a chance

Say yes say yes say yes (life can become a joyous ride)

Say yes to what ever comes your way

Take a chance don't run away

Say yes say say yes say say yes all the way all the way

Say no say no say no say no when your gut rebels

When your gut rebels trust your insides

You can tell trust you

You really knw when its yes or no

Play it out like romance

Hey it's the game of life hey it's the game of life

Hey it's the game of life hey it's the game of life

WHEN I LIVE MY LIFE OVER AGAIN – Estherleon/IvorPyres

I d say more I love you's less I'm sorries

More I need you's to really feel you

I'd say more thanks and give more smiles

For all the beauties that surround me

When I live my life over again my life over again

My life over again

With an understanding

There's something greater that surrounds me

If I had another chance I'd have more faith

Take the risk to play and dance through this life

When I live my life over again my life over again

My life over again

Searching hard to find the pieces to fulfill my destiny

And if just for one more breath I'd smell the roses

Feel the raindrops fall on my face

Knowing I have another chance

When I live my life over again my life over again

My life over again

When I live my life over again my life over again

My life over again

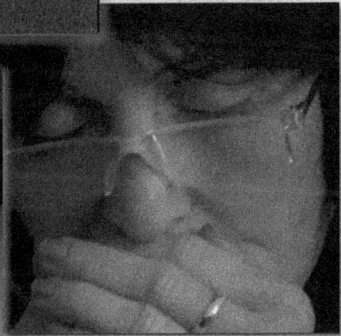

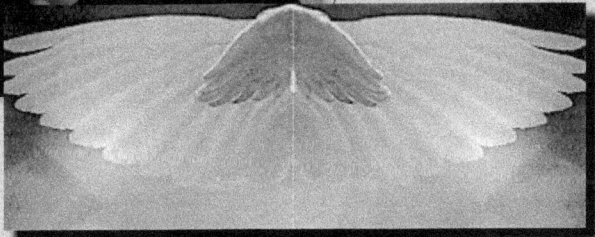

Songs written by

Estherleon and Ivor Pyres

© Estheo Records

℗ Sam 'me Publishing

℗ ChakraINK

RESPECTFULLY
diFFERENT

Estherleon & Theo

www.ingramcontent.com/pod-product-compliance
Lightning Source LLC
Chambersburg PA
CBHW030012110426
42741CB00032B/455